Enough, Already!

And Other Church Rhymes

Richard Stoll Armstrong

illustrations by
Bil Canfield

Fairway Press
Lima, Ohio

ENOUGH, ALREADY!

FIRST EDITION
Copyright © 1993 by
Richard Stoll Armstrong

All rights reserved. No portion of this book may be reproduced or utilized in any form or by any means, electronic or mechanical including photocopying, without permission in writing from the publisher. Inquiries should be addressed to: Fairway Press, 628 South Main Street, Lima, Ohio 45804.

7967 / ISBN 1-55673-544-8   PRINTED IN U.S.A.

Table Of Contents

	Page
Preface	7
Dedication	9
Poems	
Enough, Already!	11
The Campaign	13
Feed His Sheep	15
Mission Misnomer	16
Priorities	17
Keep It Cozy	18
Our Pastor Is Leaving	19
Hand to Mouth	21
The Beehive	23
Now You're Meddling!	24
If The Shoe Fits	25
It Goes With The Territory	26
With Apologies To Sir Walter Scott	27
Visitor Incognito	28
You've Grown, My Friend	30
Hit-And-Run Preachers	32
Does It Show?	33
Taking No Sides	34
User Friendly	35
A Valid Question	36

A Career Or A Calling?	37
Listen Up, Preacher!	38
Pastor's Recommendation	39
A Friendly Church?	40
The Missing Article	41
Please Don't Call Me "Reverend"	43
Knowing When To Quit	44
Sad Sacks In The Choir Loft	45
"But" People	47
"Be my witnesses ... "	48
The Price Of Irrelevance	49
What About The Rest Of The Year?	50
Whose Job Is It?	51
If It's Everything, What Is It?	53
Growing Ugly?	54
Hoppers, Shoppers, And Droppers	55
Starting On Time	56
Growth By Estimation	57
Unfamiliarity Breeds Contempt	58
Don't Call Me, Lord!	59
Wait For Us!	60
Drag On, Drag On In Gravity	61
Softer, Please!	62
Loyal Absentees	63
Ducking The Issues	64
A Lighter Touch	66

Honesty Is The Best Policy	67
When Strangers Come	68
They're At It Again	70
Go!	71
House Calls	72
Any Ideas?	73
Knee Exercise	74
Temple Tantrum	75
Where Else?	76
Depending Or Presuming?	77
This Is The Church	78
It's What's Inside That Counts	79
Who Says?	81
Surprise, Surprise!	82
Amen!	83
This Way, Please	85
Why Does It Have To Be Dull?	87
The Measure Of A Church Is...	88
Emotion Or Devotion?	89
Start The Music!	90
Free Accompaniment	94
One-Hour Limit	95
Church Bulletin Scribbles	97
Attraction Or Distraction?	99
Lame Excuses!	101
Wedding Law #1	102

Which Way To The Church?	103
Church Supper Sinners	104
Speaking Of Them...	105
Where Is Everybody?	106
When The Cat's Away	107
(Aside To Preachers)	108
Moving "Up?"	109
Lung Power	110
Hidden Sign	112
Hope For The Church	113
Index Of First Lines	114
Topical Index	118

Preface

Most of the rhymes in this collection were written to punctuate or illustrate some idea or lesson I was trying to make in a sermon or a talk. People seem to listen more attentively and to respond more positively to an idea when it is expressed in a rhyme they can understand.

Participants in the various seminars and conferences were constantly asking for printed copies of the different poems. It is largely in response to the urging of many of those who have heard the oral renditions that I have finally decided to put together this collection of poetic commentaries on life in the church.

Many of the poems have a humorous tone, often poking good-natured fun at the way church people and we pastors behave. Some of the verses are more serious, but whether humorous or serious every one of them has a message to convey or a point to make.

The discerning reader will quickly discover that the rhymes represent a variety not only of meter and style, but also of "voices." Sometimes it is a pastor speaking, sometimes a church member. Sometimes it is my own voice. In "Be My Witnesses" one of the voices is that of Jesus. It is important that the reader distinguish between the different voices, in order to get the message.

To increase the reader's appreciation of the poems and to enhance their impact, I considered including a brief description of the context in which some of them were used. After further reflection, however, I decided that it would be better to let the reader make his or her own decision as to how each poem could be used or applied. I hope preachers, teachers, and others will find them useful in their speaking and teaching.

For the so-called "average church member" my hope is that this little volume will be a source of many chuckles and maybe even a few insights. Church members should be able easily to identify with the situations, attitudes, and idiosyncrasies described in the rhymes. They are intended to be light reading, not heavy reading.

Scanning Bil Canfield's illustrations should be a delightful pastime in and of itself. His drawings bring the messages to life and lend a graphic continuity to the entire collection. I am immensely pleased with and grateful for Bil's invaluable contribution to this volume.

I am also indebted, as always, to my wonderful wife Margie, who has been my totally reliable, patiently available, and amazingly sensible sounding board and honest yet gentle critic for all my writings. She has always been the first person to read and to respond to my poems, and her constant reassurance and support have inspired my continued creative efforts.

Finally, I should like to express my thanks to all those gracious souls who have been pushing me to publish these rhymes. Their prompting has finally succeeded, and I am indebted to them for their persistent encouragement.

R. S. A.

Princeton, New Jersey

*This book of rhymes is dedicated
with gratitude, respect, and affection
to all the church members I've known,
by whose wisdom I have been instructed,
by whose good humor I have been refreshed,
by whose faith I have been inspired,
and by whose friendship I have been enriched.*

Enough, Already!

Why can't preachers, who are mortal,
    when they speak of things infernal,
know that words to be immortal
    do not have to be eternal?

The Campaign

The frost is on the pumpkin, the dew is on the grass,
    and early in November the campaign comes to pass.
Political campaigning is not what's on my mind.
    The campaign I refer to is quite another kind.

The "Every Member Canvass" it has been called by some.
    You'll know what the campaign is, when to your door they come
to ask you as a steward your heart and soul to search,
    and prayerfully consider your giving to the church.

The peacher in the pulpit can set some teeth on edge
    with but the mere suggestion that they increase their pledge.
A strong appeal for money is risky ground to trod,
    for some will always argue, "That's just 'twixt me and God!"

'Twould be a proper comment, if it were truly meant,
    but any faithful steward is wise to its intent.
And that's why some church members are nowhere to be found
    that Sunday in November the callers come around!

Feed His Sheep!

Pity those preachers who say to themselves
    "Oh, what shall I preach about next?"
Pity those preachers whose illustrations
    have nothing to do with the text.
Pity those preachers who week after week
    will constantly harp on one theme.
Pity those preachers who preach as if they
    have long ago run out of steam.
Pity those preachers whose sermons reveal
    that they haven't spent time to prepare.
Pity those preachers who love to take sides,
    but don't ever try to be fair.
Pity those preachers whose ten-dollar words
    sail over everyone's head.
Pity those preachers whose sermons contain
    no more than what others have said.
Pity those preachers who preach as if they
    are playing a part on a stage.
Pity those preachers so manuscript bound
    they can't get their eyes off the page.
Pity those preachers who never admit
    their struggles with sin and with doubt.
Pity those preachers? I guess so, but it's
    their people I worry about!

Mission Misnomer

The "Minute for Mission"
is one old tradition
our church has observed every year.
Each week in November
some well-informed member
reports on a mission frontier.

That much I don't question,
but here's a suggestion
for those who are asked to proclaim:
before you begin it
cut down to a minute,
or call it by some other name.

It's very misleading
for one who is reading
to call it a minute for mission.
When there's no abatement
to his or her statement,
I opt for a brief intermission!

Priorities

A trip to Hawaii for me and my spouse,
    a new motorbike for young Tod,
the dentist says braces for Sally and Jane,
    so what does that leave for God?

A sum set aside for the kids' college years,
    plus payments on Timmy's "hot rod,"
repairs on the house, entertainment and food —
    how much does that leave for God?

I stand for the unity taught by the church.
    I give it much more than a nod:
one faith, and one hope, and one baptism, AND —
    one dollar a week for God!

Keep It Cozy!

The fact that in a small church
    they know each other's name
is one reason for wanting
    to keep things just the same.

They think that in a large church
    they never would be heard.
And so evangelism
    is not a friendly word.

They want their church to stay at
    the size that it has been,
and they are not too hasty
    to bring new members in!

Our Pastor Is Leaving

They heard that he was leaving. They never thought he'd go.
    How could he quit this parish, when they all loved him so?
They'll miss his stirring sermons; they'll miss his thoughtful views,
    although they seldom heard him, for they weren't in the pews!

They'll also miss his children. They've grown so since they came —
    JoAnne? (or is it Janie?), and little What's-his-name?
As long as he was with them, why should they give a darn?
    "You never bolt the door till the horse has left the barn!"

To use another cliché that fits their sad goodbye:
    "You never miss the water, until the well runs dry!"
When they install a pastor, their vows they'll reaffirm
    and come to church — provided, she doesn't make them squirm!

Hand to Mouth

I baptized a baby one Sunday in May.
    For me that was one unforgettable day.
The child didn't cry or spit up, as some do,
    yet I was afraid that we'd never get through,
because when I lifted my right hand to bless,
    he did something I'd never seen, I confess.
He reached up and took a firm hold on my lip,
    and I wasn't able to loosen his grip.
I had only one hand to work with, you see;
    my left hand held him, but my right hand was free.
I could not go on with his hand where it was.
    I talked as if I had a mouth full of fuzz.
I'd pull out his hand and raise mine up, and then
    he'd get a death grip on my jaw once again.
Whenever I let go and raised my right hand,
    on my bottom teeth his wee fingers would land.
And so it continued a minute or more;
    it seemed a lot longer to me, to be sure!
Deciding at last that we had to get through,
    I blubbered a blessing — what else could I do?
Such baptism language had never been used.
    The parents, however, were very amused.
I trust that the sacrament, nevertheless,
    was valid enough for the Spirit to bless
the cute little infant I baptized that day,
    who might have been trying to help me to pray.

The Beehive

All the bees are alive in a busy beehive;
    for workers you don't have to search.
But there, my bee friends, similarity ends
    between a beehive and a church.
There is no such bee as a nominal bee —
    on the hive roll but not in the hive;
nor do they deride the beehive from outside,
    but are working to make the hive thrive.
For bees buzz around but they don't buzz about
    other bees, or behind their bee backs.
They're all making honey, not just lots of money,
    while giving themselves heart attacks.
Moreover, real bees do not sting other bees,
    as church Bs do once in a while;
nor do they pretend to be a bee's friend,
    and berate or betray with a smile.
Come to think of it, I have no right to decry
    hypocritical Bs in the pew;
for the challenge to me is the challenge to be
    and do what Bs should be and do.
So which kind of B am I going to be?
    And which kind of B have I been?
Backbiter? Backslapper? Backslider? All three?
    Or a Backer? — confessing my sin!

Now You're Meddling!

Just preach what they like
 and how lovely it goes.
The honeymoon lasts
 till you tread on their toes!

If The Shoe Fits

The truth is, to wit:
    a church hypocrite
will never admit
    "The shoe sure does fit!"
He sits there and glares,
    or vacantly stares.
She stops up her ears,
    whenever she hears,
a word that evokes
    apoplexy or strokes.

(This kind of attitude
    prefers a platitude.)

It Goes With The Territory

No matter the occasion, wherever it may be,
    if ever prayer is needed, they're sure to call on me.
To open up a meeting or bless somebody's meal
    is every Christian's privilege, and not just mine, I feel.
Parishoners should know that, but wanting to be kind,
    they turn and say politely, "Oh, Reverend, would you mind?"
Or maybe they're reluctant, not wanting to presume,
    when there's a preacher present. "That's your role," they assume.
I surely can't resent that. In fact, I want to say
    it's logical and proper to ask a priest to pray.
Professional invokers and blessers such as we
    should not refuse our clergy responsibility.
But what is quite disturbing about this lay retreat
    is that it makes us clergy "the spiritual elite,"
as if God doesn't listen to lay believers, too,
    who have as much to pray for, as we "pro" pray-ers do!

With Apologies To Sir Walter Scott

Breathes there a man with soul so dead
who never to himself hath said,
"Perhaps I should get out of bed
and go to church today instead?"

(Unfortunately, yes!)

Visitor Incognito

A visitor incognito,
    if I a phrase may coin,
I'm always shopping for a church
    I don't intend to join.
So every Sunday morning I'm
    a master of disguise.
There's not a ruse that I don't use
    to dodge those gals and guys.
I mean the ones who try to spot
    the visitors in church.
I know most every trick there is
    to leave them in the lurch.
They never see me staring with
    an unfamiliar look;
I case the joint before I sit,
    and don't go near the "book."
To make sure I'm not recognized
    I wear a false moustache,
and when the offering plate is passed
    I never put in cash,
but slip a dollar bill into
    a pew rack envelope.
The ushers think that I'm a member
    of the church — I hope!
Of course, I wouldn't dare to sign
    the church attendance pad,
despite the curling eyebrows that
    suggest that I'm a cad.

And when the blessing has been said,
    and they all stop for news,
I exit out a window, or
    I slide beneath the pews.
But somehow all my efforts seem
    to be of no avail.
The greeters still can spot me — but
    they've never made a sale!

You've Grown, My Friend

Do you feel as if your life is not just what it ought to be?
>Do you wonder if you have a right to say "Christ died
for me"?

Do you have a deeper sense of sin than you have ever known,
>and feel that you're unworthy? Then you've grown,
my friend, you've grown!

Are you seeking higher standards than you were a year ago?
>Has your conscience got a hold of you as if it won't
let go,

and made you stop and question things which once you would
condone
>or overlook? If that's the case, you've grown,
my friend, you've grown!

You've grown if, when you don't attend a service Sunday
morn,
>you really feel you miss it, and you know that you
were born

to worship God and celebrate a holy Sabbath day
>on which you go to church to hear God's Word, and sing,
and pray.

You've grown if serving others now has first place in your
heart,
>and if you've found a new desire to take an active
part

within the church and do work that you wouldn't do before.
>If better yet, you like it, then you're growing more
and more.

And what about your giving? Is it more now than it was?
>Are you giving out of gratitude the way a Christian does —

in proportion to your income? Then be glad, because you've shown
> you love the church, and that's the proof you've grown,
> my friend, you've grown.

Not good enough? Why, that's a sign that you have felt God's call
> within your heart to greater service, greater love,
> that's all.

A morbid sense of guilt, they say, is not the thing to own,
> but if you're sorry for your sins, you've grown,
> my friend, you've grown!

It's only when you've looked within that you can see above.
> It's only then you'll feel the need of Christ's forgiving love,

a love so great he gladly died upon a cross alone
> that you might live. If you can grasp this truth,
> my friend, you've grown!

Hit-And-Run Preachers

One-shot preachers have no worry;
    when they've finished, off they hurry!
No regrets, remorse, nor sorrow,
    here today and gone tomorrow!
They don't pay the consequences,
    for their pulpit-time offenses.

Hit-and-runners have it made, nor
    do they need to be afraid, for
when they step on someone's toe, they
    say "Goodbye!" and off they go! Hey,
that's not fair, for goodness sakes! We
    pastors live with their mistakes! See?

Does It Show?

We can say we love Christ with a smile on our face.
　　We can tell everybody we know.
We can share our faith stories all over the place,
　　but the question remains, Does it show?

We can put it on badges and bumpers of cars
　　and even on billboards for dough;
We can sing it in churches and shout it in bars,
　　but the question remains, Does it show?

For actions speak louder than words, as they say,
　　and faith without works will not grow.
Salvation by grace through faith is the way,
　　but the question remains, Does it show?

Taking No Sides

There are certain clever preachers
    who can cultivate the knack
of avoiding issues so they're
    never subject to attack.
If they ever face a problem,
    they will never take a side,
saying that "It's up to every
    individual to decide."
From atop their pulpit platform
    on a diving board they stand,
poised to jump into their topic,
    but they never seem to land!

User Friendly

The Bible is a user-friendly book.
   That doesn't mean it's under our control.
It means that those who through its pages look
   will find the Word is music to the soul.

Our God is very user friendly, too.
   That doesn't mean our wish is God's command.
It means that those who seek God's will to do
   receive amazing blessings from God's hand.

Should not the church be user friendly then?
   That doesn't mean it's used just to make friends.
It means its members understand that when
   they join, they will be used to serve God's ends.

A Valid Question

I have no major problem
    with church experts who hold
that churches have great beauty,
    when they are small and old.

But here's a valid question
    which they need to address:
How can one value smallness
    yet see growth as success?

A Career Or A Calling?

Is the ministry a calling or career?
    Many tend to use the latter word, I fear.
All careers are not a calling, but each calling's a career.
    The distinction isn't always very clear!

A career is not a calling if the choice
    was not made in faith and guided by God's voice.
When in choosing we're responding to the God who chooses us,
    that's a calling — and a reason to rejoice!

For some lay folks it may have to be explained
    that not everyone is called to be ordained.
Every genuine vocation is a valid ministry,
    if one's faithfulness to Jesus is maintained.

And God's call can come in ordinary ways,
    if one seeks it and is open as one prays.
Those who ask God for direction, can discern God's holy will,
    and they always want to give God all the praise!

Listen Up, Preacher!

Some ministers can dish it out, but can they take it in?
    Not wanting to be preached to is a preacher's subtle sin!
They're better at declaring than digesting truth, I fear.
    A sermon they would gladly preach they do not want to hear.

They'd rather preach to others than be preached to any day.
    They think that they already know what other preachers say.
The gospel that they travel far to preach from north to south,
    they wouldn't cross the street to hear from someone else's mouth.

There's something inconsistent, not to mention insincere,
    about expecting folks to heed what we don't want to hear.
To those who do not do what they expect others to do,
    said Jesus: "Doctor, heal yourself!" — and he meant preachers, too.

Pastor's Recommendation

I know that as a pastor
   it is certain that I'll hear
from college hopefuls sometime
   in their high school senior year.
They think it would be prudent
   if their minister would write
and help committees see them
   in an advantageous light.
But some kids never worship,
   and from church they stay away.
When they ask my endorsement,
   what do they think I should say?

A Friendly Church?

"Our church is real friendly," most members would say.
  They greet those they know, in a genial way.
They have front-door greeters who welcome you in
  with a pump-handle shake and a Cheshire cat grin.

But if you're a visitor for the first time,
  you might think that you have committed a crime;
for when you go down to the Fellowship Hall,
  the chances are no one will greet you at all!

The Missing Article

They took away the article.
They said it isn't right
to speak about THE ministry,
because one shouldn't slight
the calling of the laity
to ministry, as well.
The priesthood of believers means
we must, they say, dispel
the notion that the clergy are
the only ministers.
Whatever a lay person does
the call is his or hers
to make one's work a ministry
by serving humankind.
With that much of the argument
I have no fault to find.
But when I want to speak about
what clergypersons do
in contrast to the laity,
a "the" is needed, too.
The article implies that some
in function are unique,
compared to any unordained
church member, so to speak.
It is not parallel to talk
of ministry along
with terms like medicine and law.
What that suggests is wrong,
for it implies those other fields
are, thus, not ministry.
That contradicts the purpose of
the false theology

that took away the article!
So I for one advise
we speak about THE ministry,
whenever it applies.

Please Don't Call Me "Reverend"

What do you call a minister? Well, that, of course, depends
on what degree the person has, and whether you are friends.
A pastor's first name you may use, when you're invited to.
If not, then "Mister Jones" is right, or "Pastor Jones"
will do.
To be correct use "Doctor Jones" for one with that degree,
but just plain "Pastor" with no name is fine, because, you see,
it is a title and as such can rightly stand alone,
whereas if you say "Reverend," grammarians will groan!
For reverend's an adjective and hence it isn't right
to use it when addressing any minister. You might
have used it properly if you were speaking of someone,
and if you used a "the" (e.g., "The Reverend LeMunn").
To be more formal you may say "the Reverend Ms. Beale,"
but never just plain "Reverend" or "Reverend O'Neill."
It isn't quite as complicated as it may appear.
The problem is that "Reverend" is all we ever hear.
That makes it very difficult for folks to get it right.
The irony is that they're trying hard to be polite.
Because of that, most ministers don't mind how they're addressed,
and many clergy make the same mistakes as all the rest!

Knowing When To Quit

Those with preaching capabilities
   need good terminal facilities.

Sad Sacks In The Choir Loft

Where's the fire
in the choir?
Where's the zing
when they sing?
Why do some
look so glum
when they raise
songs of praise?
Why the scowl
when they howl?
Are they bored
with the Lord?
Are they mad
or just sad?
Why the chill?
Are they ill?
Can't they smile
for a while,
when they sing
to the King?
Showing joy
won't annoy,
shock, or stun
anyone.
They have news
for the pews
and it's good,
so they should
sing with zest.
That's the best

way to show
that they know
and they care
why they're there.

"But" People

The resident "butters" on every church board —
  what a thorn in the flesh they can be!
With unanimous votes they are not in accord;
  they'd rather be wrong than agree.

They give you the feeling you simply can't win.
  They'd vote against God, if they could.
Their forte is the one unforgivable sin:
  attributing evil to good.

Deliver me, Lord, from people like that.
  Their "butting" is driving me nuts.
"Yes, but," and "No, but" and "But this" and "But that" —
  they're sliding to hell on their "buts!"

"Be my witnesses . . ."

Who, me?	Yes, you!
Not me!	You, too!
Who says?	I do!
Why me?	You'll do.
Who else?	Too few.
It's hard!	What's new?
I'll goof.	That's true.
Can I?	Not you.
Then how?	We two!
I see.	You do?
I do.	Then do!

The Price Of Irrelevance

One requirement of guest preachers
and all substituting teachers,
if they really care how they communicate,
is to deal with expectations
and with real-life situations.
When they don't, the end results are not too great.

What About The Rest Of The Year?

Preachers who with indignation
wonder why the congregation
seem to pay no heed at all to what they say,
may have failed to make connection
with the cross or resurrection
any other Sunday than on Easter day!

Whose Job Is It?

He looked into the congregation's eyes
and told them they should all evangelize.
Discussion was more lively at that point.
Some members got right up and left the joint.
But others were polite enough to stay
and exercise the right to have their say.

"We do not make evangelistic calls!
It's in the pastor's lap that duty falls."

"Don't tell me it's the pastor's job to call.
I do not do such visiting at all.
My job is to equip you folks to do
what you as Christians are supposed to do.
Evangelism is the members' task.
If that were not the case, I wouldn't ask."

"But how can you expect the laity
to do what is the pastor's ministry?
Besides, that's what we're paying you to do.
And that applies to other calling, too."

"Not so! You pay me to enable you
to do what pastors should not have to do.
Moreover, all I'm doing every day
is true evangelistic work, I'd say.
My preaching, teaching, counseling, and such —
I really don't know how I do so much!"

That's how the age-old argument has run.
Thus no evangelism's being done.

If It's Everything, What Is It?

"Evangelism's not one thing; it's everything I do
   in classrooms and the pulpit — yes, and in my study, too!"
That's how some pastors try to let their conscience
off the hook.

   But from a Pauline point of view they need to take a look
at what they're saying when they say "It's everything I do."

   If everything's evangelism, kiss the word adieu!
If everything is, nothing is! The word is meaningless,
   and efforts to define it are just wasted time, I guess.

Growing Ugly?

If small churches are beautiful,
here's what I'd like to know:
Do small churches become ugly,
when they begin to grow?

Hoppers, Shoppers, And Droppers

Perpetual church hoppers
    can't find a church that suits.
They flit around each Sunday
    and never put down roots.

They're like chronic church shoppers,
    who say they'll join your church.
But when the time approaches,
    they leave you in the lurch.

And then there are church droppers,
    who are so quickly riled.
They'd rather leave the church than
    stay and be reconciled.

Church hoppers, shoppers, droppers
    have wanderlust disease.
Christ cannot build his kingdom
    upon the likes of these!

Starting On Time

Some pastors and chairpersons have legitimate complaints
  about the frequently encountered lateness of the saints.
Committee meetings often don't get started when they should,
  for people just assume you're starting late, and that's
  no good.
Rehearsals, weddings, classes, meals, and funerals as well —
  if nothing ever starts on time, then why obey the bell?
Those who arrive there promptly have a reason to complain.
  To punish punctuality is awkward to explain.
The level of frustration of those there is very high.
  A late beginning is a dreadful waste of time, that's why.

So here's a rule for those who wonder how to start on time.
  It's very simple, but it works. The rule is: "Start on time!"

Growth By Estimation

When their membership's declining
and attendance is way down
in comparison with that of
other churches in their town,
some smart pastors have discovered
that the best way to increase
church attendance every Sunday
is to make the ushers cease
from their customary task of
counting every single head
to arrive at the right number,
and to ESTIMATE instead!

Unfamiliarity Breeds Contempt

A frequent criticism heard in every mainline church,
    according to my scientific, unbiased research,
is that "they always make us sing those unfamiliar hymns,"
    which most assume are chosen just to suit the
    pastor's whims.
When thus accused a pastor should this one main point recall:
    "A hymn can't be familiar if it's never sung at all!"
And if that doesn't make the case, perhaps this thought will do:
    "A tune that many folks know well may be quite new
    to you,
and you might be acquainted with a text they've never seen."
    So what exactly does that loaded word "familiar" mean?
A positive solution to the problem, if and when
    encountered, is to introduce a new hymn now and then,
along with hymns the congregation has sung more than once.
    To balk at such a practice one would have to be a dunce!

Don't Call Me, Lord!

Are you looking for a prophet, Lord, a fearless servant who will stand for peace and justice in obedience to you?
Are you looking for a steward, Lord, a faithful servant who acknowledges that everything we have belongs to you?
Are you looking for a witness, Lord, a humble servant who will share the news in word and deed, as Jesus bids us do?

Fearless prophet, faithful steward, and a humble witness, too? Now that I've thought about it, Lord, don't call me, I'll call you!

Wait For Us!

The organist at our church
    makes every hymn a race.
She always sets the tempo
    to suit her torrid pace.
The fact that we can't keep up,
    she doesn't seem to mind.
The congregation's always
    about three beats behind.
Each Sunday I suspect that
    she has somewhere to go.
Whatever the last hymn is,
    she never plays it slow!
I'm sure of all the churches
    our singing is the worst.
But you can't beat our organ —
    it always gets there first!

Drag On, Drag On In Gravity

The organist at our church
    is just the opposite.
He plays the hymns so slowly,
    he gives us all a fit.
The three speeds that he uses
    are slowest, slower, slow.
The more we try to spur him,
    the slower he will go.
I do not understand it:
    Why does he have the urge
to make a hymn that's joyful
    sound like a funeral dirge?
We never feel like singing,
    accompanied by our friend.
Instead we stand there thinking,
    "Will this hymn ever end?"

Softer, Please!

There's yet another problem, which we hear a lot about.
    It has to do with organists who drown the singing out.
Ours plays so loud you feel as if your head's about to split.
    Our grimaces and angry stares don't bother her a bit.
I guess she thinks that volume is the measure of her skill.
    If she could raise decibels, she'd make it louder still.
The one advantage of our booming organ I can see
    is that no one can hear me when I'm singing hymns off key!

Loyal Absentees

When people say they're Methodists, or Baptists, or whatever, accept the information at face value, then endeavor to see if, when they say they're such and such, they actually mean it's the church they're absent from with regularity!

Ducking The Issues

From time to time issues arise that tear the church apart,
   and test a preacher's willingness to speak truth from
   the heart.
Some preachers wouldn't touch those subjects with a ten-foot pole.
   They stick to safer topics, like "Salvation of the Soul."
Then there are those who seem to be more willing to address
   the issues which have caused their congregations
   much distress.
I saw a red-hot sermon topic advertised one day,
   and so I went to hear what this bold preacher had to say.
I thought he'd try to make a case for what he thought was right,
   but what he said was not designed to challenge or excite.
He quoted other people, and although he seemed profound,
   his use of Scripture and theology were hardly sound.
And that's the way some preachers deal with issues that are hot:
   their topics sound courageous, but their preaching sure
   is not!
"This issue is important," they would have you understand,
   but when they finish preaching, you do not know
   where they stand!

A Lighter Touch

There's a ritual in our church called the Laying on of Hands.
  It occurs whenever someone is ordained.
It's assumed that every minister and elder understands
  how to do that, but they all need to be trained.

I remember what it felt like, when I knelt to be ordained
  with about three dozen hands upon my head.
As the ordination prayer went on and on my muscles strained,
  for those hands were feeling more and more like lead.

Have you ever wondered what that many hands and wrists must weigh,
  when the layers-on are leaning on one's head?
For that reason, lest some ordinand keel over while they pray,
  I have pleaded for a lighter touch instead.

Honesty Is The Best Policy

Many pastors have the notion that they have to know it all, for they answer questions everywhere they go.
To remove that awful burden and their guilt they should recall that the three most "freeing" words are "I don't know."

When Strangers Come

If you've studied your parish and know who lives there,
    and have thoroughly done your research,
you will know there are many who never would dare
    to appear at the door of your church.
To a service on Sunday they don't ever come,
    for they have no desire to attend.
But at weddings and funerals you may see some,
    who are there for a loved one or friend.
I've discovered such persons are ready to hear,
    and they listen more closely than most.
When the message is pertinent, timely, and clear,
    they will sit there completely engrossed.
Any pastor-evangelist has to agree
    that a sensitive preacher will find
what an opportune time such a service can be
    to appeal to the secular mind.
At a wedding they hear holy vows and they learn
    what a union in Christ is about.
To a funeral service they bring their concern
    about death, and their own hidden doubt.
But with some worship leaders it often appears
    they forget that those strangers are there.
They don't speak to the visitors' questions and fears,
    or it may be they don't really care.

They're At It Again

Our trustees get upset about such monumental things,
   like what to charge for weddings when the church soprano sings,
and where to put the coat rack in the basement social hall,
   and why the church school teachers have to stick things on the wall,
and how to keep the Boy Scout troop from scuffing up the floors,
   and who should be allowed to have the keys to all the doors.
Each meeting is a donnybrook, and how the fur does fly!
   They act as if on such details the church will live or die.
Such matters have their place, of course; decisions must be made.
   But things would go more smoothly, if before they fought they prayed.

Go!

If to people's homes you go,
    many will in worship show.
Church attendance then will grow,
    and your membership also.
Visiting takes time, and so
    get some volunteers in tow.
They will need some training, though.
    You can teach them what you know.
As disciples this we owe
    to the Christ who bids us "Go!"

House Calls

A house-calling pastor,
 it's still very true,
 makes church-going members,
 and loyal ones, too!

Any Ideas?

Thought the pastor in bed,
"There's a Sunday ahead,
and I haven't a topic or text."
Things are in a bad way,
when the pastor must say,
"I don't know what to preach about next!"

Knee Exercise

If prayer is essential,
    in tough times likes these
why aren't more clergy trousers
    worn out at the knees?

Temple Tantrum

On airplanes, trains, and buses, too,
    at supermarkets and the zoo,
some tots delight in throwing fits
    that drive their moms out of their wits.

A temper tantrum in the church
    would scare some preachers off their perch.
Could that be why the kids go out
    before the preacher starts to shout?

Where Else?

Such a sweet, loving couple were Charlie and Ann.
    They were always in church Sunday morn,
in the very same pew when the service began,
    where they'd sat since before I was born.
Just to see them together was always a joy,
    for whether they'd sit or they'd stand,
they were just like teenagers, a girl and a boy
    who were worshiping God hand in hand.
How distressed we all were when Ann suddenly died,
    and was buried one cold Saturday.
Even so, Charlie sat without Ann by his side
    in their pew on the very next day.
"I'm so glad that you came today, Charlie," said I.
    "What a witness you have been to me!"
Charlie smiled and then said, with a tear in his eye,
    "On a Sunday where else would I be?"

Depending Or Presuming?

We preachers claim we must depend
  upon the Holy Spirit.
That is a noble principle,
  if ever you should hear it.
It's not an invitation, though,
  for us to take it easy.
A preacher who does not prepare
  I think is rather sleazy.
There is a major difference,
  I've always been assuming,
in re our need for God, between
  depending and presuming!

This Is The Church

This is the church,
    and this is the steeple.
Go out
~~Open~~ the door
    bring in
  and ~~see all~~ the people!

It's What's Inside That Counts

There are dozens of well-packaged programs
    for inviting your neighbors and friends
to come visit your church on a Sunday.
    Do they help the church grow? That depends!
When friends come in response to an "invite,"
    if what happens inside the church door
is irrelevant and uninspiring,
    they may never come back anymore.
So before you start calling on people
    and inviting your neighbors to church,
it is always the best part of wisdom
    first to do some internal research.
Take a look at your Sunday church service:
    Does your minister preach from the heart?
Is the music enhancing the worship?
    Do the members enjoy taking part?
Is the Sunday school hour rewarding?
    Are there classes to fit every age?
Would a stranger feel welcome and wanted,
    if one came in the "church shopping" stage?
Are the programs alive and exciting?
    Is the youth fellowship doing well?
Are you deeply involved in world mission?
    Does your church have a story to tell?
These are some of the questions to answer,
    when you do your internal research.

For you want to be sure you are ready
    for the strangers who visit your church.
They may say why they came for the first time,
    and that info is helpful, I'm sure.
If they join, though, that's not the main reason.
    It's what happens inside the church door!

Who Says?

Who says I should be tithing?
   I don't like those who prod!
What I give to the church is
   between me and my God.

Who says I ought to pledge more?
   Hey! That's my turf you trod.
For it is no one's bus'ness
   how much I give to God.

Who says that what I give is
   a measure of my trust.
I'll give as soon as I have
   acquired the things I must.

Who says, "Seek first God's kingdom,
   and God's own righteousness"?
Why, those are words of Jesus!
   He could mean me, I guess!

Surprise, Surprise!

There once was a burned out young pastor,
   who did what no good preacher does.
He dreamed he was preaching a sermon,
   and when he awakened, he was!

Amen!

There was once a musician named Eric,
who persuaded too many a cleric
not to sing an "Amen,"
no, not ever again,
for a reason much too esoteric.

By arousing liturgical fears,
he convinced all his students and peers,
that they now should stop doing
what the church had been doing
for one hundred and fifty some years.

This Way, Please

Have you noticed how some ushers show
    the people to their pews?
They go sailing down the aisle without
    permitting folks to choose
where they might for some good reason have
    a preference to sit.
It is obvious some people don't
    appreciate one bit
being taken to a front pew when
    they much prefer the rear.
It can ruin their experience
    of worshiping, I fear.
It would seem that common courtesy
    demands that ushers ask
where people want to sit. Is that
    too difficult a task?
It can sometimes be amusing and
    embarrassing to boot,
when an usher loses contact with
    the ushered one en route.
I once saw an eager usher turn
    and gesture with a flare,
and discover that the person he
    was seating wasn't there!

Why Does It Have To Be Dull?

For many years I've asked around
about church music, and I've found
that plain folks don't appreciate
songs some musicians think are great.
Why don't more church soloists choose
their music for those in the pews?
The kind of solo folks desire,
is one intended to inspire,
a song that makes their spirits rise,
not just some vocal exercise.
They don't want soloists to wail
like someone practicing a scale.
Nor do they want solos that sound
like some poor howling Basset hound.
A melody that moves the heart
will stay with them, when they depart.
So many people wonder why
church music has to be so dry.
Musicians (that is, some, not all)
believe it is their special call
to raise their congregation's taste
for "better" music. They don't waste
their time on sentimental tripe.
What do they care if people gripe?

The Measure Of A Church Is...

not the great height of its steeple
    but the true faith of its people,
not its pastoral credentials
    but its sticking to essentials,
not its advantageous parking
    but its missioners' embarking,
not traditions it remembers
    but the worship of its members,
not their meaningless commotion
    but their genuine devotion,
not the lushness of their living
    but their sacrificial giving,
not their income's upward curving
    but their dedicated serving,
not what others say "success" is
    but how strong their faithfulness is.

Emotion Or Devotion?

Some church members have the notion
that their level of emotion
is the mark of their devotion
and on that their kingdom standing must depend.
Some are much too braggadocian,
and their cocky self-promotion
may just get them a demotion,
when the roll is called up yonder in the end!

Start The Music!

My sermon ended on an urgent note,
    a powerful conclusion, I had thought.
And for my closing prayer I used a quote
    that summarized the message I had brought.
It was a stanza from the final hymn,
    one that my congregation knew by heart
and now would sing with even greater vim.
    I waited for the organist to start.
But there was not a sound, and so again
    I gave the normal signal to begin
and said intentionally loud, "AMEN!"
    But still there was no sound, so with a grin
I did something I'd never done before:
    conspicuously lifting up my book,
I said, "Our hymn is number 3-0-4."
    For reasons I'll explain I did not look
to see what he was doing on the bench.
    Our organist was pushing eighty-one,
and more than once had thrown a monkey wrench
    into the works with his mistakes. No one
complained at all or showed the slightest ire,
    for he had been the greatest in his day.
Besides, he had been planning to retire
    "within a year or so," he said, and they
were old enough themselves and empathized
    with him, whom they had known and loved so long.
No longer were our worshipers surprised,
    when something in the service would go wrong.

For instance, once I stood to lead in prayer.
    No sooner had I said, "Now let us pray,"
when wham! the organ pipes began to blare
    the offertory music for that day.
He loved to take a stanza and transpose
    into a higher or a lower key.
But sometimes he'd forget the key he chose,
    and no one could discern the melody.
Whenever such a thing would happen, I
    would never cast a startled look his way,
but with a calm expression I would try
    to show what had occurred was quite okay.
I should point out that he would always leave
    the organ bench at sermon time, and sit
behind a pillar in the transept to relieve
    the pain of sitting on the bench, and it
was thus a more relaxing spot to be.
    He and I could see each other's face,
and he was hid from everyone but me,
    till he resumed his customary place.
And so this Sunday morning I had tried
    to signal it was time to start the hymn,
without so much as glancing to the side
    to see what problem was delaying him.
When still the organ music failed to start,
    and everyone was fidgeting around,
I knew I had no choice but to depart
    from that strict rule by which I had been bound.
I turned to look, and what I saw caused me
    to wonder whether I should laugh or weep.

He wasn't on the bench where he should be,
    but over in the transept fast asleep!
A moment passed before I caught the eye
    of someone sitting in the second pew.
He was an elder of the church. That's why
    he read my look and knew just what to do.
He went right over to the transept, where
    he gave the organist a gentle shake.
The latter woke, then with a startled stare,
    he pretended that he had been wide awake.
He went back to the organ bench, and then
    began the introduction to the hymn.
He was confused and flabbergasted when
    the people did not sing along with him,
because the hymn he played was not the one
    the bulletin had called for them to sing!
When he at last discovered what he'd done,
    you should have heard the modulating string
of chords he played to lead them to the tune
    they were supposed to sing. They sang so well,
that I don't want their motive to impugn.
    Was it relief or pity? Who can tell?
As for the organist, what can I say?
    After the service he apologized
to me for what had taken place that day.
    He wanted to be sure I realized
that he had taken something for a cold,
    some medicine his doctor had prescribed.
It was non-alcoholic, I was told.
    (I knew the old gent never had imbibed!)

It was that medicine, he said, "I got
   so drowsy that I simply couldn't keep
awake. Please understand that it was not
   your sermon that caused me to fall asleep!"
"It is," I said, "a great relief to me
   to know that I was not the reason why."
That worried him much more than whether he
   had made the worship service go awry!

Free Accompaniment

Why is it when we sing a hymn
    that we can harmonize,
some organists will change the chords
    and wildly improvise?

They call it "free accompaniment,"
    and that's supposed to be
our cue to sing in unison.
    Forget the harmony!

One-Hour Limit

Is it writ into law? Has there been a decree?
    Has it been canonized in a song?
How did so many church members come to agree
    that a service is one hour long?

Church Bulletin Scribbles

There's a source of information which we ministers could use,
    but it isn't one that many think about.
We would not have any trouble keeping up with parish news,
    if we had the sexton keep a good lookout
for the bulletins the members leave behind them in the pews.
    It would take the very minimum research,
just to gather all the bulletins and carefully peruse
    what folks scribble, when they're worshiping in church.
There are comments on the sermons, that we never get to hear,
    when we're greeting all our members at the door.
It can sometimes be frustrating, if the writing isn't clear,
    and we wish we could decipher it for sure.
There are funny jokes, and anecdotes, and lists of things to do,
    and remarks about the temperature outside.
There are desultory doodles and some clever drawings, too,
    and good recipes that certain cooks have tried.
There are juicy gossip items, some with intimate details,
    and snide comments re some worshipers' attire.
There are tips about new movies, and fine restaurants, and sales,
    and reactions to the music and the choir.
Now a lot of what I've written here is said with tongue in cheek,
    though it's true such doodles are within our reach.
But the most revealing aspect of this practice every week
    is the fact that some are doodling while we preach!

Attraction Or Distraction?

To every bride and groom who want some pastoral advice
   I do not hesitate to say they really should think twice
before they tell some relatives their little ones can be
   the flower girl and ring bearer, when they are only three.
What sounds like an attraction very soon becomes instead,
   a bothersome distraction that will make some faces red.
To have their children in the wedding feeds parental pride,
   but tots can call attention to themselves and not the bride.
Just watch the eyes of many persons sitting in the pews.
   The antics of the children are most certain to amuse
the wedding guests, but not the pastor or the bride and groom,
   who seem to say "I wish those kids were in another room!"
They often cry or pout or fuss and make you suffer, while
   somebody tries to tell them that they must go down
   the aisle.
And if at last they reach the front and have to stand too long,
   they wiggle, scratch, or make a face. Not that those
   things are wrong,
it's just that they're distracting to the other people there,
   who cannot focus on the service, but just sit and stare,
to see what cute or naughty thing the flower girl might do
   to everyone's amusement and enjoyment. It is true,
rehearsals can go smoothly, but that is no guarantee
   the wedding will go just as well with one who's only three.
In your printed instructions, then, insert an asterisk,
   and tell the bride and groom you think it's just not
   worth the risk!

Lame Excuses!

It's a laugh when people say
why they weren't in church today.
In the course of a church year
these excuses you will hear:
    "I work hard five days a week."
    "By the weekend I am weak."
    "Sunday is my day to sleep."
    "All the sermons are too deep."
    "That's my time to read the news."
    "They've no cushions on the pews."
    "We had company with us."
    "When we come, our children fuss."
    "It was such rainy a day."
    "It was much too nice a day."
    "It was just too cold today."
    "It was just too hot today."
    "Our old washer sprang a leak."
    "We hear Robert Schuller speak."
    "I don't like the hymns they sing."
    "I stay home and do my thing."
    "I don't have to worship there."
    "I can worship anywhere."
Lame excuses by the score!
You could add a hundred more!

Wedding Law #1

Something unusual
usually happens
during a wedding, I've found,
and if it doesn't, then
that is unusual,
if I may turn it around.

Which Way To The Church?

When they're looking for a church
 people often have to search
all around the neighborhood
 for much longer than they should.
That's a fact that underlines
 why a church should put up signs
telling people just how far
 the church is from where they are,
with directions everywhere
 how to get from here to there.
Why should churches want to hide
 from the searching souls outside?

Church Supper Sinners

For a multiple "cupper"
just one helping's no "upper"
at a covered dish supper.
So a gluttonous sinner
will not get any thinner
at the monthly church dinner.

Speaking Of Them...

To say
"They are welcome,
if they come"
means they
are not welcome,
when they come.
If "they"
are those who are
not like us,
it may
be true that "they"
won't like us.
When we
are one with them,
it will show.
If we
reach out to them,
they will know ...

... and they will show!

Where Is Everybody?

In the summer there's vacation;
in the winter, hibernation;
in the fall there's all that football on TV;
in the spring, procrastination;
that's the year-long explanation
why on Sunday some church members you don't see.

When The Cat's Away

Someone made the observation:
When the pastor's on vacation,
members of the congregation
will enjoy some relaxation
from their churchly obligation.
Now the rationalization
for their church evacuation
is they miss the inspiration
of their pastor's exhortation,
so they rest in expectation
till their pastor's on location.
But is that justification
for this glaring indication
of their spiritual stagnation?
Does their praise and adoration
cease when someone's on vacation?
What a blatant implication
of their shallow dedication!

(Aside To Preachers)

People's comments can be helpful, to be sure.
When they criticize your sermons, don't get sore.
Just remember that their comments tell you more
about them than about what you've said before.

Moving "Up"?

Why is it when a minister receives a call of God,
    so often it is to a larger church? Is that not odd?
One wonders if an "upward" call is always from the Lord,
    or whether for a job half done it is a just reward.
There's nothing wrong with being called to serve a larger church,
    so long as it's not just because one wants a plusher perch!

Lung Power

When you're baptizing a baby,
  and it really starts to howl,
you must go on with the service,
  for you can't throw in the towel.
Now, assuming that the parents
  cannot get their child to stop,
you should be prepared at any
  point some sentences to drop
from the wording of the service
  you traditionally use,
keeping only the "essentials"
  in the wording that you choose.
You cannot outshout a baby,
  and you shouldn't even try.
For the congregation loves it,
  when a baby starts to cry,
and no longer will they listen
  to the words you have to say.
And if they should try to listen,
  they can't hear you anyway.
It's amazing what lung power
  comes from such a tiny tot.
So the best way to proceed is
  just to shorten things a lot!
The child's parents will be grateful,
  if you do that, be assured,
and you won't offend the people,
  or the baby, or the Lord!

Hidden Sign

Our trustees put an outdoor sign up on the church front lawn,
   but people driving by will have to slam their car brakes on
to see the sign, because it is so beautifully hid.
   I can't believe what those unthinking church landscapers
   did.
It is a masterpiece of architectural design.
   The trouble is the shrubbery completely hides the sign!
And even if they could see it, they could not read the words.
   With its weird lettering, that sign is strictly for the birds!

Hope For The Church

There is hope for the Church
  in these trouble-filled days.
There is hope, since the One
  in whose name the Church prays
is still Lord of the Church
  and the Church cannot fail,
for he said that the gates
  of hell shall not prevail.

There is hope for the Church
  in this world of great need.
There is hope for the Church
  that will follow the lead
of the Suffering Servant
  whose good news the Church
  bears.
And there's hope for the world,
  if the Church really cares!

Index Of First Lines

A frequent criticism heard in every mainline church,	58
A house-calling pastor,	72
A trip to Hawaii for me and my spouse,	17
A visitor incognito,	28
All the bees are alive in a busy beehive;	23
Are you looking for a prophet, Lord, a fearless servant who	59
Breathes there a man with soul so dead	27
Do you feel as if your life is not just what it ought to be?	30
"Evangelism's not one thing; it's everything I do	53
For a multiple "cupper"	104
For many years I've asked around	87
From time to time issues arise that tear the church apart,	64
Have you noticed how some ushers show	85
He looked into the congregation's eyes	51
I baptized a baby one Sunday in May.	21
I have no major problem	36
I know that as a pastor	39
If prayer is essential,	74
If small churches are beautiful	54
If to people's homes you go,	71
If you've studied your parish and know who lives there,	68
In the summer there's vacation;	106
Is it writ into law? Has there been a decree?	95
Is the ministry a calling or career?	37
It's a laugh when people say	101
Just preach what they like	24
Many pastors have the notion that they have to know it all,	67

My sermon ended on an urgent note,	90
No matter the occasion, wherever it may be,	26
On airplanes, trains, and buses, too,	75
One requirement of guest preachers	49
One-shot preachers have no worry;	32
"Our church is real friendly," most members would say.	40
Our trustees get upset about such monumental things,	70
Our trustees put an outdoor sign up on the church front lawn,	112
People's comments can be helpful, to be sure.	108
Perpetual church hoppers	55
Pity those preachers who say to themselves	15
Preachers who with indignation	50
Some church members have the notion	89
Some ministers can dish it out, but can they take it in?	38
Some pastors and chairpersons have legitimate complaints	56
Someone made the observation:	107
Something unusual	102
Such a sweet, loving couple were Charlie and Ann.	76
The Bible is a user friendly book.	35
The fact that in a small church	18
The frost is on the pumpkin, the dew is on the grass,	13
The measure of a church is	88
The "Minute for Mission"	16
The organist at our church is just the opposite.	61
The organist at our church makes every hymn a race.	60
The resident "butters" on every church board —	47

The truth is, to wit:	25
There are certain clever preachers	34
There are dozens of well-packaged programs	79
There is hope for the Church	113
There once was a burned out young pastor,	82
There was once a musician named Eric,	83
There's a ritual in our church called the Laying on of Hands.	66
There's a source of information which we ministers could use,	97
There's yet another problem, which we hear a lot about.	62
They heard that he was leaving. They never thought he'd go.	19
They took away the article.	41
This is the church,	78
Those with preaching capabilities	44
Thought the pastor in bed,	73
To every bride and groom who want some pastoral advice	99
To say	105
We can say we love Christ with a smile on our face.	33
We preachers claim we must depend	77
What do you call a minister? Well, that, of course, depends	43
When people say they're Methodists, or Baptists, or whatever,	63
When their membership's declining	57
When they're looking for a church	103
When you're baptizing a baby,	110
Where's the fire	45
Who, me? Yes, you!	48

Who says I should be tithing? 81
Why can't preachers, who are mortal, 11
Why is it when a minister receives a call of God, 109
Why is it when we sing a hymn 94

Topical Index

Amen, 83, 90
Attendance: see Church attendance
Attitudes, 24, 38, 47, 48, 51, 55, 58, 70, 88, 95, 101, 105, 106, 107
Babies, 18, 110
Backsliders, 23, 27, 39, 63, 101, 106
Baptisms, 18, 110
Bible, 34
Call, calling, 36, 41, 109
Children, 18, 75, 99, 110
Choirs, choir members, 45
Church, churches, 17, 18, 23, 28, 35, 36, 54, 78, 79, 88, 113, and throughout
Church attendance, 19, 27, 30, 39, 57, 63, 71, 72, 76, 101, 106, 107
Church boards, 47, 56, 70
Church bulletins, 97
Church growth, 17, 35, 57, 71, 74, 79
Church members, 13, 17, 18, 19, 23, 35, 40, 51, 72, 76, 79, 88, 89, 95, 106, 107
Church shoppers, 28, 55, 79
Church signs, 103, 112
Church suppers, 104
Churchmanship, 17, 19, 23, 25, 27, 30, 39, 55, 63, 76, 81, 88, 89, 101, 106, 107
Clergy, 41, 43, 74; see also Ministers; Pastors; Preachers
Comments, 108
Communicating, 11, 15, 24, 33, 45, 49, 50, 63, 64, 68, 108
Congregation, 51, 58, 87, 107, 110
Congregational life, 51, 75, 79, 85, 88, 104
Criticism, 23, 58, 108
Cross, 30, 50
Emotion, 25, 45, 70, 75, 76, 89

Evangelism, 18, 28, 33, 40, 48, 51, 53, 59, 68, 71, 78, 79, 103, 105, 112
Every member canvass, 13
Excuses, 101, 106, 107
Faith, 30, 33, 37, 88
Faithfulness, 48, 59, 88
Forgiveness, 30, 55
Friendliness, 18, 35, 40, 79, 105
Funerals, 56, 68
Giving, 17, 28, 30, 81, 88
God, 30, 35, 37, 47, 77, 81, 109
Greeters, 28, 40
Guest preachers, 32, 49
Holy Spirit, 77
Honeymoon, 24
Hope, 113
Hymns, 58, 60, 61, 62, 90, 94
Hypocrites, 19, 23, 25, 38
Issues, 34, 64
Jesus Christ, 30, 33, 37, 38, 48, 55, 59, 68, 71, 81, 113
Laying on of hands, 66
Love, 30, 33, 76
Loyalty, 72, 76
Meetings, 47, 56
Ministers, 26, 37, 38, 43, 51, 66, 97, 109
Ministry, 37, 41, 51, 109
Minute for mission, 16
Mission, 16, 48, 78, 79, 88, 105
Music, 58, 60, 61, 62, 79, 87, 90
Musicians, 83, 87; see also Organists
Ordination, 37, 41, 66
Organists, 60, 61, 62, 90, 94
Parents, 17, 21, 75, 99, 110
Pastoral life, 21, 26, 39, 43, 51, 53, 67, 72, 73, 82, 90, 97, 102, 108
Pastors, 32, 39, 43, 51, 53, 56, 57, 58, 67, 72, 73, 82, 107
Personal growth, 30
Prayers, praying, 26, 37, 66, 70, 74, 113

Preachers, preaching, 11, 13, 24, 32, 34, 38, 44, 49, 50, 51, 64, 68, 73, 75, 77, 82, 90, 97
Priorities, 17, 27, 70, 81, 101, 106
Prophetic, 34, 59, 64
Reaching out, 18, 48, 71, 78, 79, 105
Recommendation, pastor's, 39
Reverend, the, 43
Sermons, 15, 19, 37, 38, 64, 73, 82, 90, 108
Servants, serving, 30, 35, 41, 59, 88, 113
Signs: see Church signs
Sin, sins, 30
Singing, 45, 58, 60, 61, 62, 83, 87, 90, 94
Soloists, 87
Stewards, stewardship, 13, 17, 59, 70, 88
Strangers, 68, 79, 105
Success, 36, 88, 109
Sunday, 27, 50, 55, 57, 68, 73, 76
Suppers: see Church suppers
Teachers, teaching, 49, 71
Time, 56, 95
Tithing, 81
Titles, 43
Trustees, 70, 112
Ushers, ushering, 28, 57, 85
Visiting, 51, 71, 72, 78
Visitors, 28, 40, 68, 79
Weddings, 56, 68, 70, 99, 102
Witnesses, witnessing, 33, 48, 59, 74
Worship services, 30, 45, 58, 60, 61, 62, 66, 68, 75, 79, 83, 85, 87, 90, 95, 97, 110
Young people, 39, 79

www.ingramcontent.com/pod-product-compliance
Lightning Source LLC
Chambersburg PA
CBHW071309060426
42444CB00034B/1742